Biogeography

BIOGEOGRAPHY

SANDRA MEEK

TUPELO PRESS

Biogeography Copyright © 2008 Sandra Meek

ISBN: 978-1-932195-70-5

LCCN: 2008926704

Printed in USA All rights reserved.

No part of this book may be reproduced without

the permission of the publisher.

First paperback edition November 2008

Tupelo Press, Inc.

PO Box 539, Dorset, Vermont 05251

tupelopress.org

Cover art: *Untitled* by Vivian Pratt

See more of her artwork at www.vivianpratt.com

Cover and text designed by William Kuch, WK Graphic Design

Tupelo Press is an award-winning independent literary press that publishes
fine fiction, non-fiction and poetry in books that are as much a joy to hold
as they are to read.

Tupelo Press is a registered 501(c)3 non-profit organization and relies on
donations to carry out its mission of publishing extraordinary work that may
be outside the realm of the large commercial publisher.

For Ray

Acknowledgments

Agni: "Grounding"

The Caribbean Writer: "Passage II"

The Chattahoochee Review: "Doolahin"

Denver Quarterly: "Idolum Naturae Magnum: A Meditation"

Divide: "Fort Zeelandia"

Elixir: "Biogeography"

Green Mountains Review: "Anniversary," "Courantijn River," "Departing Flight"

The Kenyon Review: "Fracture and Regelation Theory"

Mid-American Review: "Before De-Icing," "Paralleling the Subject"

Poetry: "Coma"

Prairie Schooner: "Cloud Cover," "The Mechanics of Failure"

River City: "Passage"

Shenandoah: "'The Supposed Degeneracy of Animated Nature in America'"

The Southern Review: "Mapping the Drift"

Third Coast: "Astraphobia," "Still Life, with *Fluency*"

Web Conjunctions: "The Ties That Bind Us," "Camera Obscura"

Deepest thanks to the editors of the above journals, to Centrum, for a residency during which some of these poems were written, and to Berry College and former provost Tom Dasher for a sabbatical which allowed this book's completion.

Contents

Chronographia

Quaternary

Theory of the Earth

On the Fevers of Our Common Country

Initialing the Grave

Chronographia

Begin at mile zero: a satellite dish
starless and webbed, great black wheel
shipwrecked to eavesdropping; a blue trailer,
aluminum skin half bricked, the man
inside tamping the trowel higher, packing in
that flamboyant faith in weather
which was youth, and winter's calm, the forest floor
littered with possibility, pine needles knit
like wishbones' twinned arms.
Break one: luck's what remains
most whole, a matchstick's matted head
before the strike, before wind's godlike finger
crooked up spring, before the trash fire
leaped to the woods, lapping up trees
as if all would be made visible
in our end. Before mushrooms, small
gray ears, bloomed in the ash, something to gather
before night's lit with the static
of remote fires and the one
unblinking star pacing the sky
catching our voices, casting them down.

Quaternary

Coma

How the body, suspended, becomes memorial
to what it used to house: wooden cross
starring the roadside; silver jet trail
expanding as it fades, underscoring then canceling the clouds'
inscrutable calligraphy. There is no shared language
between us and the night. When the truck
struck the convertible's side and sent us reeling
through oncoming cars, glinting waves
miraculously parting, what say did I have
over the words flung from me? As if *I*
broke to nothing but the teleology
of circumstance, flotsam of whatever random
predestination traffics with us, tipping the scales

so we come up *yes,* and she,
no—Tell me, as you wait
in your mother's hospital room
gone too dark to separate shadow
from body, while in the hall they debate
the ethics of respirators, of splitting the chest
to press that beat back into the hypothetically
stalled heart, where was she, as the scan
inked mourning around the brain's
one lit wing? What sound does the soul make
leaving the body? And how distinguish it
from the machine's pump and sigh, from steel
crashing against steel? But we walked

away from our wreck, days before the call
that she'd been hit; wobbly as new fawns
on the highway shoulder, grit of gravel like ground
eggshell beneath our feet, in that moment

nothing mattered, not whether we'd been targeted, spared,
overlooked, next to the crystal of broken bottle necks,
beer cans' silver spillage shimmering
in the ravine's long grass. As if that lovely green
wasn't our vision of this earth
already fraying. As if living
each day in the warmth of what would blind
if directly faced, we could keep from turning
to that brilliant, unforgiving knowledge, that the light

has never revolved around us, despite our picturing the sun
as a daily, gifted gesture. On southern
highways, styrofoam crosses mark where car
hit tree: loss hammered to a precise station,
like the one floret pricked red at the center
of Queen Anne's Lace, those stiff umbels of foam lining
the shoulder, as if in each heart the compass foot dug
too deeply in. What's a circle but a line
that can't let go? The names are what's blurred
at 65 miles per hour, and everything said is a radius spun
away from that point everything
points to, when the machine is turned off and she
breathes, or doesn't, with whatever's left of what we'd

call her will. The last of the late
afternoon light blows through the pines edging
the highway. Any two points
on a circle form an arc: directionless, and so
eternal. But the sun's dropping behind the horizon
of her window; the linear keeps breaking
through the visible world, denying the consolation of the whorls
you keep rubbing into her palm as her heart flickers
on the monitor. No comfort left, only

this: What took her breath
wasn't yours given back, what tonight you'd give
not to see her heart's handful of electric dust
falling in line across that screen.

Silver

The state of extremity, not the thing
itself, at rest: for example, wind

and light worked to whip flash from the lake's
blue-gray water; or mercury globes, spilled
metallic pearls ticking
across tiles, music

of a small dog's nails,
the thermometer's snapped neck all

fracture and glitter; fever,
unmeasured, still gathering
nests of dew, spiderweb baskets
glistening in grass, early morning; a single stone

from the freak hailstorm, what one month in the freezer
wintered from it, grapefruit
to baseball; the sky, how it so quickly can brighten
and shatter

any day's narrative, say a child
chasing a ball across a street, sun razoring
off the speeding car's fender; or history's

unanswerable light, crematorium chimneys'
great clouds—smoke or breath or the bodies' sweet
lining of soul swelling
until perspective itself, meaning

no further to go;
        a convex mirror marking the end
                of a narrow rural driveway, nailed to warn of someone
      else's hurry, steel ricocheting the zero
                even eggs trace back to
in a sliced-open hen, faintest spark

          of sheered light; hills of sheep
pushed to fog just outside
          the rearview mirror catching momentary sun
              in a foil chocolate wrapper on the road's

        graveled shoulder, sweet absence a single
              blink bright as what catches in railroad beams
paralleling the road, what appears to seam somewhere
     just a flash beyond view.

Lost Wax

What my younger face sculpted down to in your hands,
bronze I've uncloseted furred with dust (iron flakes drawn
petals to a magnet, minute feathers shorn
from a moth's steel-gray wing): another surface

to drown in. No rift or range of cheekbone, if a face
is landscape, here there's nothing
of those mountains rearing melodrama
always to our west: all profile, silhouette;

all alpine lake, encrypting the iced peaks that winter
snow kept coming down
in wide-eyed lashes. Something about process,
your interpreting hands, tracked into these facets

the fault lines that make up
a history, a weight we could turn
a dozen directions toward the light
and still come up missing

what's cradled at the core.
After any mass disaster—plane wing's stiff sail
pitched into earth, hills staccatoed
with train cars—there's always one who just

walks away, the twisted rail so like the blown bars
of his private cage—marriage, job—and the night horizon so
saturated with moon, suddenly he's convinced he could
pluck that pearl wafer, become

that irresistible light, while his name goes listed
missing, presumed dead. In the documentary your doctors finally
made me watch, caged monkeys kept pressing the silver bar
unleashing that drug chosen over food, water, companion

cowering in the next cage. Even the lobotomized
pooled on-screen kept using, craving still
flowering the brainstem at each trigger—first *the corner*
where I bought, the alley where I freebased, then any street

would do it, then *house, sun, moon,* until everything's
a trigger, and everything, in the line of fire, shining
with black ice that jackknifes the semi
through the train signal arm

coming down. Looking back makes the wreck
entire, one hundred cars a single frame fringed with prairie
and artificial sunset fading to sky a patina
of volcanic ash. Where they're melting steel to free

the buried, sparks that rise in a spray of fiery tongues
fall ash-white—marble snow from a chisel, constant
as erosion, the coastal cliffs. Looking back never turned
viewer to salt; it's what steeled her

against the burning city. The view's what's frozen,
that moment of extinguishing
perfect in preservation as the survivor walks
away from the disaster she didn't

know she'd been waiting for. No corner
to flight, the wax figure melts away to fix its form
into forever: bronze landscape shelved
on the horizon behind her, foreground all fields

studded with moon white as the houses
of the ocean's long dead, monuments to what shaped
and slipped through them, all the remains
of immersion, release.

Doolahin

Only when she stepped off the curb into the un-
sheltered storm did the car
materialize, a silver muscle of rain

thundering through her. In the hospital,
they carved the crushed leg

away from her stalled body, which felt its leaving

as an expansion of light. Dreaming,
she swaddled what they'd taken from her
in the wedding veil long

devoured by moths, in the indigo sari
she wore for Divali, the Festival

of Lights, before her conversion,
as if decades hadn't undone all but a winter's
sky of lace. What she cradled she held out

for the driver, who in the dream

had stopped, who in the dream had tears in his eyes
as he opened his arms to clasp her

wholly to him until she could feel

no barrier between her bare shoulder
and the drumming in his wrists winding down
to deeply rivered palms, long lines of life

pressed into his hands.

Paralleling the Subject

Armed with knowing the petals are invariably odd, I begin
He loves me, days I'm not looking
to reason being alone. Now it won't
stop raining. The dry creek bed out back's become the course

the world is taking, downstream. You, praying
for sun, aren't you the one who taught me
the body's a clay vase thrown
around an absent fist, who transposed
my mother's hymns beneath the staircase of any angelic

human voice? But history's the wilderness
you've wrested free of; the desert's flooded
to a mercury sheet. Winged, might my reflection
hover there among egrets, swords

of white fire, and the one hard
nail of sun, golden period stamped
after every question? As my sister's face shone
in the polished ice just
before she slipped, wrist

crumbling, discovering the body's core
a scaffold of ash, the skate's upturned blade
a silver glint, that little bit of grace
withheld.

Grounding

All night I slept
against his shoulder as they held us
stalled on a runway, powering the plane down
system by system. Restlessness is woven
into the body, vein by vein,
but even at thirty thousand feet
blood can clot and dam—*thrombosis* a bullet forged
from too much stillness, a small bird flying

hard against glass. All night passengers paced
the narrow aisle, shaking their legs to stave off flowering
into the lung a rosette of blood less slipknot
than stone, more those *rose rocks*
my parents gathered a half-century ago
from erosion, a crumbling sandstone wing
studded with iron-stained crystals
beneath the city where they'd met
years before a flawed diamond was tongued
into its knobby gold set, before the affairs, the eventual

inevitable break. Two hundred fifty
million years ago, seawater filled
that void. Beneath the skin, earth
is such emptiness, limestone's brittle lace fragile
as a sparrow's vial of bones. By morning
we'd mutinied, abandoned that broken plane
for a city I'd known only as a small
window of night, a bracelet of white lights
dissolved now by dawn. In the terminal, the man I
thought I loved told me
what to eat and when, what to say to whom

in which particular country. I was watching for wings
to silver the glass, for all the science I never could grasp
to radio in clear. How crickets
can hear with their legs. How space is really
the smallest unit of matter, and air
just another ocean, you can ride

out its currents. How the earth keeps giving up
crystals petalled in soft grit that nevertheless
outlast history, while a seagull swept into an engine
can bring a jet down. At the gate, he slept with his arms
wrapping his body. I was reading Saturn's rings aren't made
of light, but of snared moons ground to bands

of shimmering dust. That summer, retracing my parents'
younger lives, I drove past the red-stone mental hospital
where they'd worked, through what used to be
countryside, good rock hunting, now a clutter
of suburban yards, bricked fences.
What I learned from my father: it's stasis
that kills, and face cards are always
the ones to keep. From my mother: self is just

what doesn't leave you. What I taught myself
between flights, to orbit any celestial stone is to lose
everything but direction.
On the margin of a neighborhood
going up, the only roses I unearthed were failed
partial blooms: one side ridged, the other
smooth as an Amish doll's face
the maker leaves unfeatured
to avoid sin, the graven image. As if God didn't know
to go any deeper.

Biogeography

*So for the first time, we have answers to the question
of Earth's restlessness...*
—Thomas E. Hemmerly, *Appalachian Wildflowers*

Reading landscape again fails me, having lost the necessary
nomenclature of wonder, both family
and scientific names. Distant kin to Narcissus, I expect to find

myself in every local habitat, in spruce-fir and cove hardwood forests,
bogs and balds, cedar glades: I've traced the breakage
of history's stone tablets to illustrated field guides

cleaving fossil, mineral, animal. The safety in numbers
is in their division: Cherokee, Seneca, Micmac, Catawba; monocot
and dicot; whatever's exiled, trailed

to tears, accounted for. Even this evening no
continuous fade but an extinguishing series
of blue equations, each shade measured by how far it's fallen

from day's *sky blue*. Though nothing stalls
continental drift, the weathering
mosaic of the body, serpentine barrens where the soul,

like any soil, composes itself by horizons, layers visible
only in profile. The terror's in facing
anything head-on. Better to note the way distance

breaks the forest to layers
of aspiration: shrub, understory, canopy.
In geologic scope, what the ground we're mesmerized to won't

let us forget, these mountains are a single
inflorescence, a half-life not more than one
exhalation of stars. This is the ice

we skate, clarity
which brings us down; genesis
of binomials—second naming of all the transitory's

incarnations, flora to fauna—that craving for return
to the earliest garden, as if again what was left to us
was world enough, and time.

Theory of the Earth

Anniversary

To become air, you say, think
one hand clapping; the doomed oak's
desolate fall; or how the river
beneath this bridge transfigures
drought's puzzled mudflats
to motion, the rippled map
of desiccation channeling the turtle's neck
arced just beyond the streaming dome
of her known world. But the body's adrift
in *when*, saturated with *since*. All nature
a modification of water, parchment
for rain. And this November sky,
this near-pearl field of weather
propelling ghosts from the river's
skin? One more failed surrender
an oak leaf's clawed hand pinwheels
along the current, nothing but gravity
bearing it down.

Before De-Icing

What embraces
brings you down: my hands, God's
hands, moist and freezing. So much

for Elizabethan grandeur. So much

for music: those crystal spheres shattered
to confetti, glitter's mute scales drawn

to the snowglobe's ground zero,
our shining skin. Earth's skin, wasn't
that history, broken

to its smallest divisor? Or some
braiding in the bone, belying all law

of superposition, the way our rising

won't mean *eternity*, won't mean *future*.
The past bubbles up

in volcanic veins, in repeated
dreams: your archetypes are my
inscrutables; my familiars,

your blurred question marks. The future, any
glass sky, prone

to splintering. Waiting's become

the absence of clarity: Air, galvanized
to childhood's milk, to a white

craving. As every question ends
in itself. As the one drowning

dragged her rescuer
beneath the broken ice, climbing his body
mid-lake. Having lost all faith

in horizon. And the view descending
so lovely, silver blades rotating

in gray air.

Event One

We spread across the temperate world as if it would last
forever, while millennia's held breath

        bubbled Greenland ice flowing surface-
forward, an extended

glance of light. Our climate's history is clocked
        in beetle casings, the thickening skins
    lakes secret, articulations

of the body. If stars don't destroy us, weather

will. We are its children. What calmed
        six thousand years ago stopped

    the wandering; cities
were born, and alphabets, Word as landscape, and climatology, the theory
                    of our eminent end

at the hands of ice. This far south, in Georgia,
        pockets of air are what's left when groundwater's drained
    by quarries and drought. Overnight

        a sinkhole opens; morning, the earth's
    a cupped hand holding

its own broken bones. Camp Century lasted
a decade. It was the cold war. Ten top-secret years
        counting layers of summer and winter snows

like an abacus of tree rings spiraling
                    toward an origin perhaps itself

nomadic, moving
            through *us,* what it whips up to veil
its one stormy eye, a Ouija's

                glass window guided by whatever
is writing us down.

138 feet, Atlanta
            is burning; 2500 feet down, Socrates sips hemlock.

Blackened here by Pompeii ash, here by Roman smelters' lead,
                ice they're again drilling no longer
            registers sublime without that lost

theory of doom, not global warming's
                slow slippage, but *what can calm
can craze again,*
                climate like science fickle and owing us

nothing. Time, for now, remains

a weight. One hundred thousand years down, pressed snow
                    is ice, and materiality
            a ticking; brought to the surface, the sample

                may explode, like the heart
of a diver, too quickly risen. Camp Century's now

part of the drift—mess hall, hospital, skating rink, shelves of perfume
                for absent loves, all

scatter and flow beneath a night sky stippled

        with ice and dark breaths: absence knocking

   between heartbeats, the sound a word makes

when it's taken back.

Cloud Cover

Repeating the experiment makes it true, makes it
science, this string of gray days

its own conclusion. Each one a needle, a hummingbird sipping
something sweet away. Every

childhood December, cedar waxwings, drunk
on fermented crabapples, dove into the bay window,

demonstrating *not sky* one by one. Frozen smoke
of a failed season, the one pondering

the possibility of *dissolve,* the row of icicles set trembling
didn't fall. Far

from the neighborhood, the lake beckoned, crystal fist hovering
at zero, grained and gritted knuckles

buried in earth. What weather taught: milk breath
on the pane meant *self,* what clouded

ice crystals swirling like ringworm come alive
beneath the doctor's hand, black light urging its entry

into the visible. Eight months a year we lived
in winter. The forty words for *snow*

someone else's and too far north, each morning a silence
circled my bed, something coiled

like a fingerprint in the corner of that gauze veil
a fly's jags and halts wove high

in the ceiling the moment just before
waking, when *I* is both line and spin, the needle unthreading

music from a record's engraved disk. Before
the inevitable descent into the pane

of the body, a length of *only* like a name
inscribed on an i.d. bracelet (what you were

to give away to
signify love), indelible as eternity

snagged into symbol, figure eights skaters still keep carving
into that lake.

Camera Obscura

From Emerson's "Nature"

It is like a great circle on a sphere, comprising all possible circles; which, however, may be drawn and comprise it in like manner. Every such truth is the absolute End seen from one side. But it has unnumerable sides.

—Ralph Waldo Emerson

Hand of the mind,
     this zodiac of light, this tent of dropping clouds,
     the angular distinctness of objects conspire

          to emancipate
   the animal Eye, Immortal pupil—A face of country
quite familiar, history

well compared to snow: fire, wind, water, the law
     of arches, the mariner's needle, range
     and scale, all the epoch of one

degradation: inch by inch vaulting
the thick darkness, focal distance arranged under the name
          delineated on air

        unrealized at once, matter
like an outcast corpse—An evening knowledge
     unfixes land and sea, makes free the solid

seeming, postpones the apparent order, *vespertina*
cognitio, mountain stratum where granite
        is differenced—

Things are ultimates   a single sex   I
a trifle   a disturbance   glad to the brink of fear   rudest crystal:
Where would it stop, this resemblance

to morning, this striped coat of climates,
this fourfold year, fountainpipes on the unfathomed sea,
Nature aloof, afloat: the street, a puppetshow—

Refractory world, immortal Necessary,
the whole circumference of man an appendix
pure and awful, wonderful congruity

to wander, bell and plough
radically alike, the pantomime of brutes
(ocean of air, of water) who converse

in figures, typing the human hand
in a fossil flipper, *saurus*—
Every new law of color gleams

of a better light, nature
underfoot; the doctrine of Use, dwarf iron face magnified
to first principle: *I*

break, chop, impoverish   I
prefer imperfect theories   the universal tablet
deep calls to deep   the ruin
our own eye—

The Ties That Bind Us

Are ligneous, muscular, chemical...
—Jane Hirshfield, "The Lives of the Heart"

Are igneous, sedimentary, metamorphic;
are made from dawn silk, hedgehog bristles
of hemp; double as jump ropes, window bars, satin
handcuffs. Are aquatic, earthbound, angelic.
Scatter deer, grow shy among rabbits, meet coyote
dead in the eye; resist reciting
the fourteen lines of the heart. Embrace Flat Earth theory.
Change glass to stone, to fire;
empty villages, cover everything
with fine ash. Make their own seasons, rain needles
at midnight, crack oak ribs with crystal;
break stone fists with silvery roots;
embroider our solitude. Draw lines in the sand that are
always shifting. Lift the hot air balloon but then
remember the earth. Anticipate
angels, vultures, whatever arrives
in the end to clean up. Glow as amber
numbering the dark. Speak in hieroglyph, cuneiform,
tags of graffiti; call to us in dreams, fall
mute on waking. Take shelter
in sky writing, stalagmites, pennies
pressed on train tracks. Hold us
to distance, to gravity. Wander away
in crowded malls, refuse to accept their names
in intercom timbre; cast stones
in still pools, observe in widening circles all things south,
cul de sacs, pirouetting ever-afters. Enumerate
the colors of birds, declensions
of insects; calculate solar eclipses, play only

black keys. Fail to grasp photosynthesis, the doctrine
of signatures, genetic code. Are tone deaf; offer
flawed interpretations, human
sacrifices, castles of air; read the body
as parable; view hands as smoke.
Are architectural, amorphous, primordial
with history and grace. Shift continental plates, rivers'
courses; bridge synapses. Are all that
pushes and pulls. Are all that fades,
that is interminable. Tether
the astronaut, erasing the enormity of space. Fall
too quickly to earth. Postpone
the night, whatever unravels us.

Fracture and Regelation Theory

Where species overlap (sympatric, simpático), songs evolve
                              and diverge, no *I* without *you*
            distant, or strange—so this fallen male I hear (a female
                        would be nearly silent, a mere
                              wing flick)
                              low in the bush, his body's fluted drum

what sings, not the flawed wings' scrim of rain meshed
                  in black wire's lace, what crowding or chemicals' fine veil
            twisted, trapping him (*dogday cicada, harvestfly*)

in flightless emergence. Late summer
                              is a vibration of air, the world
            humming; my observation, the field
                  where row after row of the chemically mutated

line up, pin through thorax, pin
                              through thorax—My freeze
            doesn't fool him; he cuts off,
                              stranded
far from the canopy's chorus evolution
meant him to reach by blood's
                        hydraulic extension inflating and

lifting his wings. As amulets of jade, secreted
                  under the stilled tongue, once they marked hope
            for rising, the past misting away
                              to a scarf so transparent it

can't be seen, finer even than that cloth before the weavers' thumbs
                              were amputated, a crimson sari pulled entire
                 through a wedding ring, finer than the soul

blooding the body, that delta of iron, of rust, vein
                              to capillary: the rivered earth
            in aerial view, dendritic map
                 of the valley grained in the trunk beneath the crackling

abandoned skin: *Magnolia grandiflora,* its own range
            narrowed and pared (climate change,
                              glaciation) while beetles droned
                 after huge, moon-white flowers, acorns going off like distant
buckshot in the reservoir—

                              All things near
in their loss. Sun in the fist of trees, chapel bells rack up
                 the elegiac number while the dying goes on in un-

memorialized silence and the dead drift
            into overgrown margins, scrub
      of sumac and pine,
                  flicking their failed wings—

Idolum Naturae Magnum: A Meditation

—From Gorman's *Philosophy of Animated Existence*

In space rich—Beautiful for its worlds—the immensity
of Matter hinges

without reasons. We decompose
to be present, take for the Whole

the great Mutation, vast and frightful solitude
as our better fortune. Living empire, coeval

to our ecliptic course, witness duration
in the Doctrine of Lost species; breathe

as we are Breathed, without decay
or diminution; Unburn

the visible horizon, Invisible universe—distance between
ever be infinite.

On the Fevers
of Our
Common Country

Karma

More than one stillness
fists the heart: the coconut palm's bronze

cluster of fruit ripening
towards earth; the *picolet* caged to sing

back the forest to its brighter self
winging there. *Brotherhood,*verboerderig,

it was just a phrase, the retired
revolutionary laughs, *something to keep*

everyone sleeping. A jaguar bounds
across the road, its coat a field of black eyes

haloed in light. The only tapir I saw
lay quartered and bleeding out

in a turquoise canoe. Lotusus stood by, opening
enormous red hands.

Astraphobia

I play the recorded storm each day notched higher
for the dog thunder sends crashing through window blinds'

contrived calm, horizon strung again and again
against our view. Terror must be erased
by the distilled music of terror. The president says *terror*

twenty-nine times in his speech. Lines in the sand multiply
across the desert's wrist, the typical become beautiful
as electric light born in a glass fist's crosshairs
at the flick of a switch—

When weather returns, it's vision
that panics her: polestar become meteor, western sky arced
by failure—lightning's flash an apocalyptic wing
razoring the room with its

erratic pulse, pounding her heart
to the tremble of the rabbit she once

cornered in the yard. Not thunder, light's
covert shadow mushrooming
through sky like this morning's contrail

dissolving to cipher: I had no translation for the sentence
that narrowed as it neared flight, spidering
to hairline fractures frozen across an eggshell
cracked as finely as the palm

to its fault lines. Inside, cool

unattainable air: you can't get
in without breaking
the way out and therefore failing

to escape history writing itself in exhaust
above the lake lined
with newly bloomed trees, spring's
ghostly architecture made visible

bone by hollow bone. When the word is needed, the book
falls open to the page. Cities

crumble. So tell me the sky

isn't falling when this morning the clouds
cauliflower the lake's pocked green glass,
bottled pine. Latex gloves dragging missing fingers

across the sand, wind raising waves like hands signing
stop even as they crash ashore

moons of styrofoam packing
now scattered in morning glory mimicry
along the spillage ditch. Clean,
scooped sockets, flowers of the familiar

to end with: that old drugged sleep, her paws rowing
a dream I imagine skyed with fields of plump,
furred creatures, their legs divinely
useless, and on her back,

The Mechanics of Failure

The day began with what airplane pilots call 'severe clear':
seemingly infinite visibility.
                    —David Remnick, "September 11, 2001"

Jumpers, we called them, as if no nerve, no marrow, still held
to flight, as if falling

wasn't in the blood, and even today the long
habit of light might not

be broken, torn
to gold laces like yellow ribbons

tied around oaks for the hometown hostage who finally
did return, blinkered

by camera flash, one year after
the warm June evening I was married, absurd

in formal white, beneath those noosed trees now
too easy to read in curling photographs

as *caution,* as *remember's* thread
wearing each swelling trunk to that familiar

arc of pain. Mostly
there is no warning: planes slam

into buildings, or you do your own
crash and burn, lighting life down

to a finger of ash. My ring, removed,
left a groove that took years

to vanish, what seemed scar finally
a fading, the way, after seasons, a grave settles itself

into earth, or a winter day's flock of starlings
does stop pouring east, though all morning

their crepe banner had seemed
horizon itself, the blackened sun still

enough to burn the watcher's eyes
to the gold of its own sightless image, the faith

in vision what blinds. Despite their knowledge
of velocity, despite their ability to calculate

the gravity load of the cell, the fire load
of bone, some held plastic sheets, makeshift

parachutes, as they dropped, as if the world
wasn't wind, and fist, and whirling fragments

of paper; as if what we're falling from
isn't grace, isn't what,

a century ago, the newly arrived believed
they could recreate, releasing

one hundred European starlings to populate
this world new and strange

to the Shakespeare they'd read
as home, setting in motion this morning's

rolling eclipse, five million birds in one gathering, one
city of flight; so when from the 100th floor, yes,

they did jump, the question, how much of our weight
can this world bear, had already been asked

as a storm of dark wings, a wake of gray light
streaming behind.

Wealth of Nations

Blind now, the dog retraces her path
door to water bowl; water bowl,
door; until the muscle's mapped, she has it
by heart. So much has gone underwater
to keep the lights on. Whole villages
of grass. Regiments of terracotta soldiers
swimming in sand, centuries held in clay

dissolving. When the Suriname
was dammed, the wildlife rescue
failed, and how many
drowned, *monki-monki,* toucan,
jaguar? Live traps

remain empty, and attic mice narrow
the roof over our heads, insulation a fur
each night thins. In the dark, even blood
jewels. The failure of alchemy
gave rise to *goldstone* my twice-widowed aunt
works into necklaces, copper crystals glittering

that muddy field. The dead
radiate data, what medical schools coveted
two centuries ago to fix
human organs into something
to steer by, bodies of light constellating
night sky the wealthy hired
watchers against for each beloved newly
flooded with earth. Two weeks' decay, and thieves
abandoned the body to eternal

profitless rest. Watchers descended
the tower's spiral steps I climb
searching for my father searching
among stones for the famous economist's
engraved name in this city of steps he's still
mostly able to take, his elder sister far
down the hill with her two

new knees. Married to a ham radio man
at twenty, she tapped Morse to Finland, heard
first of Sputnik in code, found her husband still
belted to the roof's huge antenna, heart
exploded in his chest as her mother's
later would, spilling her room

to a startling ruby. When I kneel
to sweep prairie grass from my grandmother's
marble marker, a cocklebur's star of needles
catches at the fan of veins
purpling my ankle. Towers of storm clouds
clot the horizon over what was

my grandparents' farm, now Kentucky
blue grass and Arabian horses, fields a green deeper
than memory's cotton. My father never found
Smith's grave. Everything he knew of theory, that
invisible hand, it took us

nowhere. Underwater, Suriname's rainforest,
China's earthen armies. Towns
of crumbling silos, the southern
valley. Underwater, doors into familial earth
that faced sunlight so bright to make
out the letters your shadow had to fall
through the hollows of each carved name.

Passage

Our plane spirals beneath mountains steeped
in forest and copper-rusted zinc, Port au Prince

a bone maze focusing not
to promise's scaffold, the new

going up, but to the unfinished
in ruin, unroofed rooms

housing vine sprawl and palm. Our stop
unscheduled, simply

to refuel, we stall out
away from the terminal on the runway's

cracked and pitted plank, and it's as if we were still
looking down at the ridges

we'd sunk into, not at this patched tarmac
but blackened islands in a sea our arrival has washed

color from, turquoise to sapphire. Mica
shimmering the tips of gray waves, sun

ground at our feet. These windows offer only
the illusion of commerce

or communion: this near visible air
weighted with rain, with sea, never

enters my lungs, never gloves
my body; is shaped only to the plane's armor suit

cast from our final destination, the continental forest
shrinking in reverse alchemy behind the company sign, *We*

Move Mountains, the factory's huge
concrete legs, earth stripped for bauxite

so in our aluminum skin we can
rise over the forest to view

that tattered green. Accelerating
down the rippled runway, we lurch

like a small boat, rough waves racing
against shore; at touch off, we

are voiceover, erasing all
local articulation as the plane's cross x-es out the land

blurred below. What we give back: the blindfold of shadow
flickering like a raven flying just below

the island's skin, a root ripped up in one
fluid motion so the black soil hidden deep

below this exhaustion, overturned,
briefly rises, then Haiti

is swallowed again, sealed
by a roof of clouds which clears to a chain

of unnamed islands, earth's knobbed spine,
knuckles of white sand, stranded.

Passage II

Then the red roofs of Curaçao
                                erased, trays
           carried down aisles: plantation rum and Coke,

such sweetness bled from cane. Towels to staunch
                              the unexplained drip
           from the compartment above my seat,

like water wearing down stone
                         or the forehead of the one
           who refuses to speak, leaking from whatever breakage

we've carried with us from home. As if height
                        granted dominion. Engines spill their silver
           banner of smoke to skies over the country we are to land

in, where a ribbon's hung from the hook
                       where they found the body
           within the walls where slaves' resistance ended again and

again with the rack and the whip, with roasting,
                       with quartering: with, for one, an iron hook, with
           hanging, not by the neck, but by the wing of bone

inside his split chest, his case unusual only
                       for his witness's horror, who noted
           how, *suspended alive,* he caught with his tongue drops

of water *streaming his bloated breast,* how this kept him alive
                       three days, how he spoke
           only once, to upbraid the youth who cried out

as he was flogged beneath those gallows, calling

down to him, *Are you*

a man? It was the rainy season, it is

again. Forest-green, hand-blocked in black letters, *Recht en Warrheid*

maken Vrij, the ribbon's already moldering

in that cell in a colonial fort still guarding the river

the forest—greenheart, purpleheart, mora—is floated down, limb
by broken limb.

Fort Zeelandia

Suriname, 2003

Twenty-one years, and no one has answered
for those knocks in the night, for Leslie,
for Josef, for thirteen others

cut down to symbols
of dissent, for Sourendra riddled
as sign, lead weighting his chest

in a shattered cross, for their voices hushed
within these walls still laced
with slaves' last breaths. Time

will tell nothing of the stars
the army plucked to stipple the olive skies
of their shoulders, unhinging thigh,

hip, from foreign gods still
constellating the night. The moon, thrown
into relief, more deeply pitted, more

like this fort wall, clean sockets
bullets bit into stone. What's left, the shooters' view:
shore's far green gesture; sapphire

and grace, the wake of a small boat
arrowed toward dock, delicate
as a coin cutting glass, a finger signing fog

breathed into a mirror. Because morning
doesn't bring clarity. Distance
isn't perspective. At ten paces

anyone can vanish, revolution a spinning
toward eclipse. What can't be seen
from space: the Great Wall

crumbling, coral reefs
boiling to oblivion, subway cars dumped
off the New Jersey coast, trusting

the lungless will rise once again
to revise the rust. Some stories can be told only
in oblique revolutions, a dark cell's

memoriam: blackened lamp,
a steady thumbnail of light until the oil
bleeds away and the wick flickers down

to a tongue of white ash. The smell of salt
and toppled forest rises
into rain, the coastal breeze

soft as moss already weaving
velvet of this chipped stone. The centuries' cataract
museumed in glass, apothecary bottles etched

with skulls and crossbones: danger
as fair warning, the gun cocked on the shelf
of the arm before the final view

from the wall. Arcing above clay tiles, just the scalp
of flambouyants, a shock of red blooms sprayed
across the shivering green.

Courantijn River

Breathe in, and you are that clarity
cradled before word, before the fracture
between *rainforest* and *jungle:* transparency
our small boat hummed toward, away
from the brackish coast, a town
of rice, white waves of egrets a tattered flag
rippling before tractors, palm-lined canals choked with algae
and lotus a red deep as the heart
tongued open. Heartwood, what mangrove lacks
levitating low tide, ornate signatures rooted
in the sweetness of salt. Such perfect balance, such

perfect revolution: the eldest son lights
the pyre, the old man burns on shore. Mangrove
raises up the salt, sweats fine crystals from leaf tips drenched
in sun. It isn't true fire is weakened
by light: even in tropical noon those flames
eclipsed the white sand slowly shrinking beneath the sea's
unraveling hem. In the capital, revolution is a marble frieze
erected amid the blown-apart police headquarters'
surviving pillars, a beautiful woman in flowing
stone robes, that archetypal
iconography, not mother or lover but virgin

blessing the men's guns, the *waterkant*
she faces. Rivers
are roads in this country, whole villages exist
only by water. Four hours into the forest, we landed
in the village Independence was to have flowered
to a second Paramaribo. An engine of rust and leaf
stranded near the *stelling* where we docked—

the track's steel backbone, wood crossties laid
like a xylophone's ascending scales, disappeared
in the green, music
never struck; even the small monument I stumbled
on, its gushing inscription dedicating the *Opening
of West Surinam,* nearly lost in emerald's
cursive scrawl, those same vines villagers hack

to free a day's path. Maybe you've read
how mangrove spread across this world
simply by floating—Kashmir survived as the blue
of his eyes, milk and honey and Krishna, the blue light
of God, dipped into the *panch amrit* the widow offers
each pair of cupped hands. Cane
now entirely fringe, the sugar fields
are ready to burn. The cattle have stopped dying
of old age in the grass. Who's left to bury them
with ceremony as they fall? The slaughterhouse,
she says, is kinder than carrion carrying off
those soft eyes in their claws.

Continental drift, the earth as steeled plates
crashing together—however you read
the history of the planet, it all scopes down
to points of ash, small fires dotting a forest village
to keep the bush down. *Next time you come,*
Sohan says, *Apoera will be bright bright,* meaning
the mine will be open; already the men are here
digging ditches for cables; already a clearing, a satellite dish
cocking its ear, hooked to the harbinger,
the one working phone villagers keep arriving at

on bicycles. Already the local prostitutes are overwhelmed
despite the men's general shrug, *they all have AIDS.*

The former dictator's party initials
paint the walls, the imported American pine
at the guesthouse where the men overnight. Another election
in the works. The night after talking
to the woman whose lover was tortured
and killed for his writing, I dreamed a head
entirely face, eight eyes encircling the skull, each

stabbed out. In the forest, every little boy carries a machete.
Things grow so quickly, the green springs back so fast
without fire, without the *earth-mowers* the mine
is moving in. Kan-kan, mahogany, purpleheart—
   everything that shades us
will be cut down. In the city houses go up in
anonymous flame to keep witnesses quiet; the crumbling
remains of government buildings burned long ago,
left standing. No one forgets. What they saw
was two decades ago; this year the national census
went up in flames, two torched warehouses. Held as they were
only on paper, the name of each citizen
extinguished—

                Try holding
your breath, try saying nothing as everything comes down
around you. Close your eyes: even in bright sun, the world is milk,
cloudless. Listen: do you hear the teeth
approaching, do you trust the light, how it eats equally into
shadow and green? Have you noticed? The body without air goes blue
letting in the sky.

El Dorado's Mosquitoes

Imagine an island embedded
in a continent of smoke, bright nugget

to bite through to: metal heart
encrusted with wings, songbirds and crepe blooms
dissolving to dusk's swarm: *the devil's*

trumpeters, pin-snouts tipped
to lance wrist and cheek, each

a stitch of burgundy sipped from the slack
faces of the dreaming
bruising rain-battered earth:

Imagine sky closing down
to stammering grid points, the darkening
canopy mapped with humming arrows circling

a penciled-in X, the only constant

its shifting as it homes
the glister of *farther*, of *furthering*

the faith, crosshairs which set sail
ship after ship, imagine an ocean churning
to froth erasing

word from mouth as mind or soul or
whatever was self

plumes away, a puff of smoke abandoning body
to arrival and fog creamy as the reputed

milk of paradise heralding
each landed sunrise and sky a vast
river, imagine,

stoned with gold, bright as the stars
bleaching away with night, nothing but violet

left to steer by.

Theography

The little rainy season: meaning the storm
resurrects itself a dozen times daily
as rain without thunder, malleable sky

matching the sea's twilight
phosphorescence which itself transliterates
to Mother Ganga's gold comb glinting

starlight among the waves, that amber
translucent liquid offerings timbre down to
on spirit-house altars. Gold chains make the body

an offering to angels. Air veined and humming
with outsized dragonflies, moon a powdery
half-thumbprint pressed into the pale

blue throat of morning—pyre
or crematorium, the body burns
three hours to ash. The first drink goes to the earth

each time a vodka bottle's seal
is broken. Once you've landed that buttery shore
you don't come back

from the stars, the rice fields slowly
draining just as you've become fully
a creature of water. Herbal baths render couriers

invisible to police; inside them balloons of white powder
sleep like children. Deep in the river, piranha, fantastic
caricatures of hunger, slide beneath net-

fed waters where the succulent catch
and sparkle with fight. What they know
about us: the human brain is a fist

white with need. You must obey your guardian angel
to keep him with you. When you find Mother's
sparkling comb, you will dream the secret

to wealth and happiness, and where to return the comb.
Somewhere among these rocks is a golden key.
Somewhere among these rocks, a heart-shaped hole.

Initialing the Grave

Last Passenger

How enumerate flight, move
beyond *many,* dark *wing, advent*
of blackened pearl: Earth
receptive to shadows. Billions
in a single flock. We swung

the sun's bare bulb over
our shoulder, nothing to break
light's fall. Material only
as a candelabra of antlers, deer
slung to trailer yoked

to sixty miles per hour down
a freeway equals
the rate passenger pigeons reached
at cruising. The left lane's
open. Our speed

a single arrow west.

Mapping the Drift

By law, southern colonists raised mulberries, a sheen
silkworms spun to sleek winding cloths,
body casings unraveled to thread
women wove to clothe children now woven

into this earth sprouting *shepherd's purse, beggarweed,*
evening primrose a green an *anole,* American
chameleon, has matched exactly, the hunt a stillness

sculpting him as second stem until, crossing
so easily into a predicted future, he darkens
to burnt umber, shade of the dying *doveweed*
he steps onto, disappearing once more

into this battlefield where I've traced myself
back to the great-great-great-great Carolina
grandfather who fought among the ancestors

of these blighted pines. Don't we all long
to become the view? To be drawn
into a treed world we can never be certain who
called us to, though my father's grown sure

the body broken beneath this cairn
will rise whole again, even the cremated gathered
to a resurrection beyond our understanding, it will be

that true. I just want to get down
the chameleon's stiff dance, his lurching
leaf-mimicry, the way light breaks
across the lake, all toward, no

arrival, how, having given up on time, cemetery stones
green with moss read only *In Sacred Memory*
of beneath carved lambs, my own sad elation

on finding the names, Moses, Agness,
beginning to rise from marble into dusk's
blue smoke just beyond the church founded
two hundred and twenty-two years ago on the then

frontier, border between revolution
and genocide. So much
we can't call back. Wired

for linear determination, the thread unwinds
generation to generation. To mine, where the name
rubs out. I traveled as if that name
listed in battlefield rosters, lined in stone, could illuminate

conversion, how he stepped so easily
into belief, into language rayed
directly from God, *in tongues* a rapture

unexplained by learned allusions this landscape
keeps calling forth from him, carrying, as his father
before him, that leather-bound book only
in old age. Family history's a drift west we compose

to the beginning of memory: Oklahoma, the dustbowl,
his father sharecropping cotton. The law
kept failing. The silkworm industry

didn't pan out. People kept moving, changing the rules.
Revising rock's distant spillage in ice, mists steaming
this browning grass. Science, like history, a letting go
one theory to step into another, abandoning

the nebular hypothesis—once-boiling world cooling
toward ice and shadow, absolute zero of all life
erased—for global warming, heat unexplained

even by July, the South. Humidity brings ink
back into my hand brushing the page, heat
blurring the categories, making my body more
memory of the lake, the way light faltering

across its surface makes the lake a more
familiar uncertainty. Only the observer witnesses
how successfully the stem

is duplicated, not the chameleon who knows
he's matched the view only by what he is
able to catch, what fills his belly,
which one theory has

as the pit of the soul. Walking
away from the cemetery mimics time's dissolve
to a screen of ash and bone, pearl buttons

milky as the toadstool still holding
the chameleon's shadow ribbed with fine
unwritten parchment, the smell
of mold, archival paper tracing a name

to disintegration and mildew. Nothing
doesn't fade. Nothing
doesn't go hungry and unanswered

into night haunted by a sun which may or
may not be signaling
its own dying in that flawed

and welcomed light.

World as Nocturne

And its movement seemed so terrible, aglitter
in its glass bed, that he stretched out in grass shaggy
with pine needles, made the turquoise haze of morning

that summer's key tone—eighteen,
dropped out, getting high in City Park
where this evening a woman pushes her life
past in a shopping cart, her child dropping into his hands
a gnawed man of blue plastic she'd finished

toying with. Terrible the movement
of memory, of the mind, how what I'm thinking
even as he tells another woman his story, even as,
replaying it, I stumble through this
awkward cadenza, is how I want to hold him

in every inflorescence—man, teenager,
boy—to place my fingertips against his forehead
like a magnet to compass-glass, scattering true north

in all directions. Desire's an overreached octave
pearled free from everything that
no longer matters. This late in life, we only just
glance off each other, and Chopin's rhythm
is complex: five in the right hand against

three in the left. It should all come together
in the end. But Chopin died young, and so much
is out of my reach: the rare

plumage of birds; arpeggios that once
sped through my wrists; the one broken pane
above the altar of the church where
at eighteen I gave my sole
solo recital. My own years stoned at the park

were over by then. Each day
was broken to music: practice, theory,
composition I never

could finish: first movement, a motif
weaves hand to hand; second movement, and the body's silk
parachute flutters just beyond sunrise, the rim
of arrival—but again I'm overwhelmed
imagining history, how it holds to the future, the third movement so

easily modulating to the sweet nothing
of letting go. From the piano, from the altar of eighteen, if I'd turned
back toward the darkened chapel, I almost believe
I could have touched him.
At this distance, he almost fits in my palm.

Departing Flight

I promised I wouldn't, but I watched you
weave the ribboned maze all the way
to security, point beyond which
I couldn't follow, gate and ray so powerful
if unshrouded it would flare
into the marrow, the body's
deepest secrets. *Tell me*

a beginning, you said as we huddled
away from travelers stranded
between two storms. When I was four,
my mother reached to replace
the light that had sizzled

away from its crossed wires, to change
that milked crystal to a touch
of her own fire. I thought the failure
to become light had made her
cry out, not the slipping disk I

learned of later. When I was four I learned
loss is the other side
of grace, speed that scattered
the full bag of popcorn I'd propped
in my tricycle's basket. Faith

is like that, feet on the pedals
birthing wind, a small storm spitting
spectacular snowflakes.
Because science was what I
couldn't grasp, I imagined the soul rose paling

every evening's sky, that flying you aren't
really rising with nothing
to hold you, the planet's arc
meeting sky in severe clarity not more
fracture than seam. What I wanted
to tell you was there's always been a world

of laws beyond me and I would have broken
all of them to cool that small burning
inside you, to sweep away those vials
of pills, your ritual circle
forecasting ash. What I'd magnified
to harvest moon telescoped
so smoothly down to a loose quarter I'd wish
into any fountain for you, silver flash always

beneath the water. Even the skeletons
of gods drawn around stars break down
to odd bits of stone; a comet's just
when there's no distance left
between fire and ice. It's earth
that claims us. I know my body will become
its own fist of blown glass, you the sweep
of light my camera first

caught of the stars
left open all night in my grandparents'
unelectrified yard. That all
the hurricanes will leave this far north
is a deep blue lingering. What I wanted to tell you
is betrayal, like tragedy, is in the acting, not

the act, that my life before was nothing
but a held breath, that driving north

toward home, you far beyond
the gate, I finally saw the horizon's hem brighter
than reason, that boxed light
erasing our faces' dance

scrolled onto film. What I wanted
to tell you: the story of beginnings is always
God as a ray of light
too brilliant to bear, too brilliant
to turn away.

Still Life, with *Fluency*

Fort Worden, Washington

Penpoint gunnels slip invisibly
through eelgrass meadows: evolution, that long
attention to place, narrowing,
greening their bodies to the paper-

thin blades of home. *Fluent:* no border between
self and word, no distance
between elements, water's *fluid* and fire's
flue, its channel out of the house

veiling a valley already
silvered with fog. *Zostera*
marina, a forest canopy, sinks with the rising
tide as when *America* spread

wildfire across the continent's last leg and *disappearing*
guns rose above parapets only at the moment
of firing, cranked up on carriages
above the bunkers' Belgian concrete poured

with local water flowing
into land, by sea: a trick of vision
lost to the march, war's
technology of motion—airplanes

and submarines rendering coastal forts useless
as the balloon company encamped in wind
slapping seasick the soldiers stationed
in gondola baskets. Nothing

but practice: gunpowder sheathed
in silk-lined canisters; guns loaded with sand
fired at rafts set adrift like paper
cranes in the Sound, the Strait of *Juan*

de Fuca, a Greek who disappeared
into his sponsors' language. Nothing but azimuth
and range, thirty corrections
before aim: curvature of the earth; deflection

for drift, angle of departure; slope
of fall. Nothing but watch and wake
while in Europe guns were loaded
on railcars, bombs made to be dropped

by hand from wooden triplanes
bandaged with canvas. Men
in *companies* lined up under
single letters: *F* begins *fire,* ends

bluff. Hard places to hide: hunkered down
on a concrete bunker, noon
longer each day, shadow a small wing crushed
beneath each gunner; open sea, life

silvering toward transparency
not to be targeted, jellyfish both window and soft
poisonous shell. Survival of the fittest, meaning
the least seen. What blends doesn't bleed, we want

to believe that. When radar was invented
(to make up for echolocation,
attention, some missing sense that
would have guided us under water

or air, some camouflage to wear
the world on our backs even as we disappeared
into it), symbols for kelp and eelgrass were
already blurring on navigational maps like the edges of fine

colored ink tracing territories in the first
blueprints to *discovery,* melding to one
ambiguous sign. War no fort against air
charged with microscopic breaths of

unheroic destinies whispered into the ear, *flu*
killed soldiers by the dozens at this stronghold
at the end of a war which ended nothing
but the Roman numeral I. The lull, safety

at its most dangerous, any word repeated—*love,*
sorry—risks becoming
another kind of silence. A sudden twitch
in the eelgrass gives the fish

away; something inside you matches
nothing in your life, nothing in the words
twisting your tongue more tightly
into their net. No chart

of corrections. No hostile ships
in the bay. Just the one ferry
crossing and recrossing its heraclitean path setting off
from coastal shallows, eelgrass beds rooting into

flowing earth. Landscape of sandbars
and depressions, low tide exposing the forest
in its trench like those dug-in soldiers as the first planes
droned over, how on a day clear

of gas, one looked up at his own
certain death which still arrived to him as a winged
bolt from the blue, tossed by a hand
lost to all that azure.

Om, with Kelp and Crows

Sinuous as an eel, a single blade
ripples, a fluent

fluid fin fanning the wave's dark
spillage and froth, an oil-slicked grebe

tumbling to pulse,
erasure. The view from the cliff

gravitates shore's ruffled wing to the spectrum's
counterpoint poles, bridal lace

and widow's crepe: surf's tatted hem
an alpine blaze; crows a serene

midnight glance, what wakes
without us. On the beach, clarity's

lost to vision, all things flock
toward gray—ivory quill paling

each sleek feather's spine; inky water shadowing
every wave's curl. Scattered

in sand, litter of stones
ground smooth as lingams

pearled on shore, each crow-foot's print
is Shiva's trident tangled

to repetition, three still points and what's held
dual at the core—emptiness

the heart of flight, emptiness
the float, bobbin that buoys the kelp

nearer its food, the sun. All arrows point
to their own circling, *murder* a family name

more us than them. What a syllable's held
millennia scientists

finally believe: the earth
does hum—the sixty days a year

without earthquakes they hear it
always from winter's pole, North Pacific or Brazil's

southern coast, migrating
against the birds, filling

that absence of wings. The planet's plates
are always flexing, edges

rippling like a shallowed ray,
a bay encircled by

barely breaking. A shrimp caught above tide
spirals between rocks, one small

margin of terror. A mountain boils
to the south, readying

to blow. Crows' beaks scooping through sand,
kelp stipes rising

eight feet each day: hunger
muscles the neck, stretches the body

toward the light, the unleashed
dog scattering birds

in tatters gusting up like boot-blacked
newspaper scraps, sending them hunting

along the surf, flight a black thread sewn
to its own unraveling.

"The Supposed Degeneracy of Animated Nature in America"

Honeysuckle lathers its way up silver maple, black gum,
sumac: slipped free

from the garden, home became the fallen world—fences' refusals
to erase, to flower upon. The theory

was everything new is everything we'd loved—even as it flickered

away from us—in decline: travel telescoped
to correspondence and regret, landscape

to mirroring disappointment we visioned as God's eyes, cast down on us
until we turned back to tasks, speaking *wilderness*

into a continent, nearly making it so. This, when word

was act, when what lacked a name
lacked place, and what cast no shadow

had no soul. But all landscape is the record
of migration, these trees having fled the wilderness of ice

flowering behind them, what seemed beauty

an invasion, deliverance. Outsider, how you must work
to be loved, stitching yourself

continually into view, persuasion's green archetype tongued
with butter and cream: how you would

kill for it. Each new bloom's a bride's glove, removed to receive

the symbol of union, what's absent,
here, what might shimmer just this near the palm, mapped,

as any of these net-veined leaves, with private flight diving
into the wrist throbbing with voices

stifled because the word had already been spoken

and splintered, and what appears two
separate waves of color, milk

and honey, is
an illusion: each white flower yellows into its own

forgetfulness, what makes it

fall, what restores it to the garden
beneath—what so much belief in beauty

has nearly exterminated—revealing
the empty socket on the stem, the blindness always there

at the heart of flowering.

Notes

"Quaternary": Quaternary is the geologic period during which humankind has existed.

"Doolahin": Doolahin is a Hindi word for bride.

"Event One": I am indebted to Elizabeth Kolbert's article "Ice Memory" (*The New Yorker* 1/7/02) for much of the information in this poem. The term Event One refers to the "instant ice age" some scientists believe ended the last interglacial period; validating Event One would be tantamount to proving Earth's climate is not merely subject to gradual change, but is radically unstable, suggesting a similar sudden disaster is likely in the planet's future.

"Camera Obscura": This poem is made entirely of words and phrases from Ralph Waldo Emerson's essay "Nature."

"The Ties That Bind Us": This poem is for Jane Hirshfield and is after her "Lives of the Heart."

"Idolum Naturae Magnum": The poem is made entirely of words and phrases from John B. Gorman's *Philosophy of Animated Existence, or, Sketchs of Living Physics with Discussions of Physiology Philosophical, to Which is Added a Brief Medical Account of the Middle Regions of Georgia* (1845).

"On the Fevers of Our Common Country": The phrase is John B. Gorman's.

"The Mechanics of Failure": David Remnick's article, "September 11, 2001," appeared in *The New Yorker*, 9/24/01.

"Passage": *Recht en Warrheid maken Vrij* is Dutch and translates: "The right to justice and the right to truth make all people free."

"'The Supposed Degeneracy of Animated Nature in America'": This was the title of botanist Stephen Elliott's 1791 valedictorian speech, rebuffing the theory of degeneracy, a theory which, as Alexander Wilson put it, "would leave us in doubt whether even the Ka-te-dids of America were not originally Nightingales of the Old World" (*A Sketch of the Botany of South Carolina and Georgia,* Stephen Elliott).

Find These Uncommonly Good Tupelo Press Books
at tupelopress.org or call 802-366-8185

On Dream Street	(2007)	Melanie Almeder	$16.95
The Animal Gospels	(2006)	Brian Barker	$16.95
The Gathering Eye	(2004)	Tina Barr	$14.95
Mulberry	(2006)	Dan Beachy-Quick	$16.95
Bellini in Istanbul	(2005)	Lillias Bever	$16.95
Cloisters	(2008)	Kristin Bock	$16.95
Sincerest Flatteries	(2007)	Kurt Brown	$ 9.95
Modern History, Prose Poems			
1987-2007	(2008)	Christopher Buckley	$16.95
After the Gold Rush	(2006)	Lewis Buzbee	$14.00
The Flammable Bird	(2006)	Elena Karina Byrne	$14.95
Masque	(2007)	Elena Karina Byrne	$16.95
Spill	(2007)	Michael Chitwood	$16.95
Signed, numbered limited edition hardcover*			$100.00
Locket	(2005)	Catherine Daly	$16.95
Psalm	(2007)	Carol Ann Davis	$16.95
Signed, numbered limited edition hardcover*			$100.00
The Flute Ship "Castricum"	(2001)	Amy England	$14.95
Victory & Her Opposites	(2007)	Amy England	$19.95
Duties of the Spirit	(2005)	Patricia Fargnoli	$16.95
Calendars	(2003)	Annie Finch	$14.95 (pb) $22.95 (hc)
Ice, Mouth, Song	(2005)	Rachel Contreni Flynn	$16.95
Mating Season	(2004)	Kate Gale	$16.95
Do The Math	(2008)	Emily Galvin	$16.95
Other Fugitives and			
Other Strangers	(2006)	Rigoberto Gonzalez	$16.95
No Boundaries	(2003)	Ray Gonzalez, ed.	$22.95
Time Lapse	(2003)	Alvin Greenberg	$22.95 (hc)
Keep This Forever	(2008)	Mark Halliday	$16.95 (pb) $21.95 (hc)
Longing Distance	(2004)	Sarah Hannah	$16.95
Inflorescence	(2007)	Sarah Hannah	$16.95
Numbered limited edition hardcover*			$100.00
Invitaion to a Secret Feast	(2008)	Joumana Haddad	$16.95
Night, Fish, and Charlie Parker	(2006)	Phan Nhien Hao	$16.95
The Next Ancient World	(2001)	Jennifer Michael Hecht	$13.95
A House Waiting for Music	(2003)	David Hernandez	$14.95
Storm Damage	(2002)	Melissa Hotchkiss	$13.95
Red Summer	(2006)	Amaud Jamaul Johnson	$16.95
Dancing in Odessa	(2004)	Ilya Kaminsky	$16.95
The Garden Room	(2006)	Joy Katz	$ 9.95

Abiding Places, Korea North and South	(2006)	Ko Un	$16.95
You Can Tell the Horse Anything	(2004)	Mary Koncel	$14.95
Ardor	(2008)	Karen An-hwei Lee	$16.95
Dismal Rock	(2007)	Davis McCombs	$16.95
Signed, numbered limited edition hardcover*			$100.00
Biogeography	(2008)	Sandra Meek	$16.95
Bright Turquoise Umbrella	(2004)	Hermine Meinhard	$16.95
Why is the Edge Always Windy?	(2005)	Mong Lan	$16.95
Vacationland	(2005)	Ander Monson	$16.95
Miracle Fruit	(2003)	Aimee Nezhukumatathil	$14.95
At the Drive-In Volcano	(2007)	Aimee Nezhukumatathil	$16.95
The Imaginary Poets	(2005)	Alan Michael Parker, ed.	$19.95
Everyone Coming Toward You	(2005)	David Petruzelli	$16.95
Darkling	(2001)	Anna Rabinowitz	$14.95
The Wanton Sublime	(2006)	Anna Rabinowitz	$16.95
When the Eye Forms	(2006)	Dwaine Rieves	$16.95
Bend	(2004)	Natasha Sajé	$14.95
Approximately Paradise	(2005)	Floyd Skloot	$16.95
Selected Poems: 1970-2005	(2008)	Floyd Skloot	$17.95
Distant Early Warning	(2005)	Rad Smith	$16.95
O Woolly City	(2007)	Priscilla Sneff	$16.95
Every Bird is One Bird	(2001)	Francine Sterle	$13.95
Nude in Winter	(2006)	Francine Sterle	$16.95
Embyros & Idiots	(2007)	Larissa Szporluk	$16.95
I Want This World	(2001)	Margaret Szumowski	$13.95
The Night of the Lunar Eclipse	(2005)	Margaret Szumowski	$16.95
In the Mynah Bird's Own Words	(2002)	Barbara Tran	$9.95
Devoted Creatures	(2004)	Bill Van Every	$14.95
This Sharpening	(2006)	Ellen Doré Watson	$16.95
The Way Home, A Wilderness Odyssey	(2004)	Bibi Wein	$16.95
Narcissus	(2008)	Cecilia Woloch	$ 9.95
The Making of Collateral Beauty	(2006)	Mark Yakich	$ 9.95
American Linden	(2002)	Matthew Zapruder	$14.95 (pb) $22.95 (hc)

* Proceeds from the purchase of these limited edition books help to support *Poetry in the Schools*, a national initiative that brings working poets into elementary and high schools across the country.